Stepping Up
To The Plate:

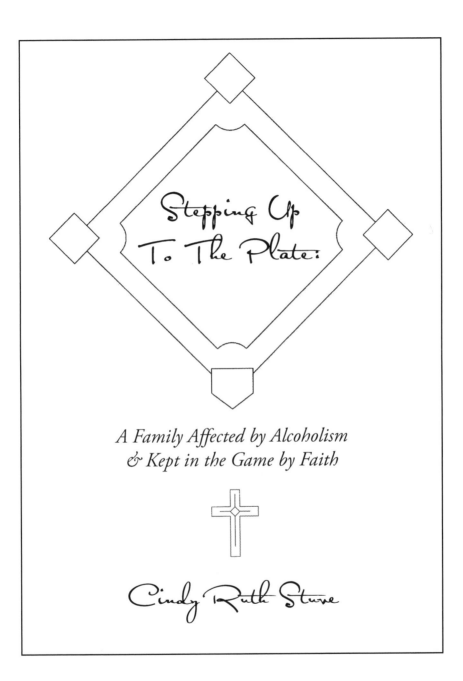

Stepping Up To The Plate:

A Family Affected by Alcoholism
& Kept in the Game by Faith

Cindy Ruth Sturve

authorHOUSE®

AuthorHouse™
1663 Liberty Drive
Bloomington, IN 47403
www.authorhouse.com
Phone: 1-800-839-8640

Published by AuthorHouse   04/04/2012

ISBN: 978-1-4685-4060-4 (sc)
ISBN: 978-1-4685-4059-8 (e)

Interior book designs courtesy of Elizabeth Anne McKern.
Interior book photos courtesy of Andrea McKern.

Church photo permission granted by Collegiate United Methodist Church and Wesley Foundation.

DEDICATION and PRAYER

Dear God, Thank you for always
being with me in the game of life.
I continue to pray for all families and friends
deeply affected by alcoholism.
I specifically pray for each member of my family
as they break down the ancient ruins
(generations of alcoholism) for themselves.
I pray my sons and their generation
can see beyond the glass castle ideal and
are able to build healthy, loving, responsible,
strong and manageable lives of REALITY.
I step up to the plate honored to be your mother
by dedicating this book to you,
my greatest life blessings, my three sons.
I love you with all my heart, Mom

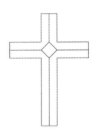

1 Corinthians 13:13
[13] And now these three remain: faith, hope and love.
But the greatest of these is love.

STEPPING UP TO THE PLATE:
A Family Affected by Alcoholism
& Kept in the Game by Faith

By Cindy Ruth Stuve

TABLE OF CONTENTS

"We cannot tell what may happen to us in the strange medley of life.
But we can decide what happens in us . . . how we can take it,
what we do with it . . . and that is what really counts in the end."
(Courage to Change. One Day at a Time in Al-Anon II)

CHAPTER 1

Opening Pitch—Understanding Why

My parents met in the 1950s while in high school in Rock Falls, their hometown. Dad was a basketball player and Mom loved the sport and that was part of the attraction. He was a couple of years older and went on to play basketball and attend the community college in town. When Mom was just 17, they started their married life together and by the time they reached the ages of 22 and 20, had three children. I came five years later. I don't remember us as a family—all six of us together, which I truly regret. Although they were young, my parents, Rick and Betsy started out on fairly stable journey. Dad earned a teaching degree and took on a teaching and coaching job in a small town in the Midwest. Life was pretty normal. Mom cared for us while Dad worked, and we had many friends in our little community. It was fun being a coach's family, according to what my family has said. There were some great times and good family memories.

Fast forward to my adult life looking back . . . I (Cathy) am the youngest of four children (one sister, Nancy, and two brothers, Bill and Seth). I write as the daughter of an alcoholic father whom my mother divorced when I was only five years old. After our lives began to fall apart, Mom divorced Dad, took a factory job, and raised us on her own. My dad, Rick Nelson, committed embezzlement and went to prison. He let alcoholism overcome him and never found his way back into the game of life. I have a faint memory of an aunt and uncle taking us kids to see Dad while in prison one time. During our childhood in Rock Falls, he would breeze in and out of our lives and we never knew where he was or how to reach him. As I child I never understood this. Why he didn't step up to the plate to help raise us? Why didn't he provide for us or pay child support? Didn't he love us or care for us? How could he leave Mom with the burden? How could his way of life be more important than being a father to his four children despite the marriage ending? Why did he not want our family life? Did he not realize his responsibility? For most of my childhood I searched for a way to understand.

While Dad was teaching and coaching, a friend of his from Rock Falls called one day and gave Mom a message to pass along. The friend made Dad an offer to come work for him and he accepted. Our family returned to our hometown of Rock Falls while I was still a baby. It was here that he took on his new accounting position, which eventually led him to the embezzlement. I wonder if our family life or this game would have been different if he had not taken that position. It is a good question. Mom told me she even wondered herself if things would have been different had she not told Dad about the call. I believe Dad thought he had to come back and "be somebody." He was pretending to be something he was not and tried to prove himself to his peers in the community and wanted to make it big. That may be when his escape from reality began: buying rounds of drinks uptown when he was in no position to do so with a wife and four kids at home.

Since I was so young, I don't remember all that my siblings do. But what I do remember is not pleasant. One of those was being outside on the sidewalk one day and hearing my parents fighting and being so scared because I could hear the sound of breaking glass. By the time you reach the end of my story, you will understand the symbol of that one particular memory. Another time one very late night, I was asleep in my room but woke Mom and Nancy screaming. They had locked themselves in the bathroom and someone was trying to break in. I realized it was Dad but I didn't know why they were scared. I kept still and prayed quietly that he would leave. I didn't understand anything at the time or for many years. He must have eventually left because the only outcome I know is my realization years later that he must have been really drunk that night and that is why they were afraid.

I was lucky to have my grandpa Walter Cane in my life; we all were. I remember him attending father-daughter events with me so I would not be alone. This meant the world to me. I know that Grandpa played a huge role in helping us through this difficult time, as well as many others. I was honestly too little to understand much, but I know my sister and brothers remember some pretty painful times that not only affected them as children, but also as adults, and sadly all of us for our entire lives. I was heartbroken when my sister told me she used to cry in the bathroom stall at school because all the gossip was so upsetting to her. How could it not be? How can you explain inappropriate behavior in adults? Why do we have to try? Why don't the adults realize the damage they do to children?

Over the years we would hear stories of Dad being found asleep in the local park in town or seen hitchhiking along the highway. Other times we would hear that he was all the way in California. None of it made much sense or seemed real to me as a child and I never understood why. One time as a teen as I was in the car with Mom and she said, "There's your father." He was actually hitchhiking along the side of the road. I was driving and it really shook me up. She said she was sorry for startling me but it wasn't her fault. It was the reality of Dad's life; I had just not seen it so clearly for myself until that moment.

When I was in my early twenties, Dad, my sister and I participated in family counseling, which was a choice for us but a requirement for him as a result of more trouble with the law and his alcoholism. I remember complete strangers in our group therapy, after hearing about our relationship, asking why my sister and I were even participating, we owed him nothing. But we were brought up in a family of love and we had each other and our faith. We were giving him a chance to make up for his absence in our lives and helping ourselves try to finally understand and to cope with all the damage. It was then that I truly began to understand the reason for everything that had happened. It was because my father was an alcoholic, but I didn't understand it during my childhood. It was the reason he was not a part of our lives. I finally had an answer. It didn't have anything to do with his loving us or not loving us, but more about his love for the drink and lifestyle that went along with it. During this counseling, as young adults, my sister and I were able to confront him with our anger and pain, and I will always believe it helped us work through it and move on. I don't think my brothers ever truly dealt with all we went through and I also believe it is the basis for my brother Bill's own alcohol addiction.

Drinking has never been an important part of my life. As a matter of fact, I am probably just the opposite and could actually live without it completely. I have never been one to let myself drink extensively even in my teen and young adult years. Maybe I have been too reserved. Maybe I am missing out on something everyone else seems to enjoy or has to have, but I don't think so. I enjoy an occasional glass of wine or a mixed drink but that's it for me: one or two is enough. I don't ever want to lose control of myself or my life even for one day. Maybe there is a reason my drinking habits are reserved and I am thankful that I realize that there is so much more to enjoy in life and am able to step up to the plate when necessary.

Philippians 4:7

[7] And the peace of God, which transcends all understanding, will guard your hearts and your minds in Christ Jesus. (Biblica)

CHAPTER 2

Team Favorite—Love in Our Family

Usually every sports team has a player who is the fan favorite. In our family, I think that person has been my oldest brother Bill. He was always popular and our family home was the place to be during his high school years. One thing I have always known is that we were on our own a lot. We all (my sister primarily) had to grow up too quickly and carry responsibilities that most kids don't. Mom's factory job had alternating shifts and often overtime. She definitely stepped up to the plate for the four of us by having this job, but when my mother was at work, my sister was often left in charge. I know my sister felt the extra burden, but she did what she had to do and I will always be thankful for the role she played. After my sister went to college, I went from having just two big brothers to being the popular little sister of all those gals and guys who came to my brothers' parties! In high school my brother Bill did drink a lot and was lucky to have made it through some close calls, but he wasn't really doing anything that his peers weren't. But, I will always wonder if he would he have escaped alcoholism if there had been a father stepping up to the plate for him in those years. Or, was it bound to happen to one of the four of us? It is interesting to see which way kids of alcoholics go—toward it or away from it.

I have always been proud of my brothers for how hard they have worked to raise their families despite not having the example set for them. How do you learn to become a good father when you grow up not having one in your life? My two brothers were very active in the childhoods of their kids and did so much for them growing up. I believe that all of my siblings and I have worked hard to do the best we can for our kids. We knew we didn't want to let our kids down the way we had been: a goal for all of us was to be good parents. I know Mom's life raising us alone was not easy. We were also fortunate to be supported by our grandfather Cane and the love of our Aunt Penny, Mom's only sister. Many of our father's brothers and sisters and their families were also very caring to us over the years. I continue to be in awe of the character of people who step up to the plate when it is not necessarily their turn at bat. At the same time I find myself questioning the character of those deeply affected by alcoholism, and their inability to realize that they should pick up the bat. I get it—it's the *disease*—but how many players have to be hit with it in one family? And why aren't the alcoholics ever the ones to see it?

After high school my brother Bill found a job with a family-owned company in our hometown and worked his way up the company ladder. I believe he became an engineer without the degree. He married a local gal, Elaine Jens. They were a well-known couple in Rock Falls and had many friends and family members living close by. They were blessed with two incredible sons whom I treasure as my first-born nephews. As our family grew, so did my brother's popularity; his sons adored him, all his nieces and nephews from both sides of the family loved him, including all my boys. He was the center of FUN at many family gatherings—he was the guy to play with, tease, climb on top of, and the list goes on. Yes, he was the fan favorite of our family team! Good old Uncle Bill! At age four, my oldest son broke his leg at his birthday party just because he wanted so much to be a part of the FUN football game that my brother Bill and his sons were playing. Unfortunately he came down at the bottom of the pile!

I have always thought that the four of us—Nancy, Bill, Seth and I—loved deeply and remained strong for one another in life, since we didn't have that father figure and were on our own a lot.

I think we all would have done absolutely anything it took to help each other out and often times we did so. The love we felt for each other as a family among us, as well as the love from others, was always apparent, but we still sometimes had misunderstandings. I believe that my sister resented having to be in charge when so young. I know that my brothers were angry at Dad, even though they never expressed their feelings. I know I just wanted everyone to be safe and happy, so sometimes my lack of understanding of it all caused me to withdraw. I also had the added burden of adjusting to Mom's second marriage and being part of a stepfamily. My siblings were older and out on their own so able to move on.

Elaine, Bill's wife, and I were always close. I cared for my nephews when they were young and I was a teen or young adult. Later on, as our kids were growing up, my family would often stay with Bill, Elaine and their boys. Elaine and I discussed our concern for Bill's drinking problem many times. During one July 4th celebration, Bill wanted to take my boys uptown to the carnival while it was clear he was not sober enough to do so. I hated not trusting my brother, but it now affected the safety of my children. I couldn't allow it. Every year when we were together during the Fourth of July celebration, something unfortunate would happen related to Bill's drinking problem. I was often Elaine's confidant—little did

I know that someday I would be playing the same game myself. We discussed a family intervention many times, but only Elaine, Mom and I believed it was the right thing to do, not my sister or my brother Seth.

Bill is an alcoholic, and I would say that sadly, he has been one most of his life. "Alcoholism is a broad term for problems with alcohol, and is generally used to mean compulsive and uncontrolled consumption of alcoholic beverages, usually to the detriment of the drinker's health, personal relationships, and social standing. It is medically considered a disease, specifically a neurological disorder" (Wikipedia). He often made the loudest negative comments at his son's sporting events and was kicked out of numerous games. My heart ached for his boys when this happened. I believe every family member loved Bill so much and voiced our concerns from time to time, but nothing really worked. So, we continued to pray, we tried to move on, and we tried to let go and let God.

One time we took a bus trip when Bill and Elaine's son Mark was playing college football. I watched my brother start drinking at 6:00 a.m. and he wasn't alone. Watching it, I just knew the day would not end well. Mom and I were in tears and actually held hands on the trip home when things got ugly among some of Bill and Elaine's friends. And yes, alcohol was the reason for the scene. If only people could see themselves and the effect of alcohol on their behavior. When we got back, everyone went home except Bill. He was always the one. I even cried and begged him to just come with us and asked him why he can never seem to get enough. He didn't reply and went on to the bar. His actions seemed to play out, just as the definition of the word alcoholism stated, ". . . to the detriment of the drinker's health, personal relationships, and social standing." That night he got home safely somehow, as he often did, and life went on.

Over the years, Bill had one personal DUI (driving under the influence) charge and a work accident that injured a coworker and totaled his work vehicle. He was not charged, but I do wonder if his drinking the night before played a role in the accident. There have been many sad stories of people seeing him at bars or at football games staggering drunk and even wearing soiled clothes. My brother was sick; he didn't have cancer, but he was an alcoholic. Shouldn't we be willing to step up to the plate for that disease too? I kept telling myself that I was willing to do all I could to get him the help he needed. He desperately needed help—his alcohol consumption was out of control and his life was getting worse. He was even kicked out of a college football game for going on the field in a drunken state. I told Elaine in every conversation we had over the years that I would do anything to help. Mom had said the same, and one time she shared with us a beautiful poem she had found called "Standing In the Gap. It was a beautiful piece. But all the words, the love in our family, our prayers, our pleas or our tears—none of it was ever enough to help Bill. What would it take? Would it happen before he hurt himself or others?

Standing In The Gap

I'll stand in the gap for my son
I'll stand till the victory's won
This one thing I know, that You love him so
And your work with my child is not done

I'll stand in the gap every day
And there I will fervently pray
And Lord, just one favor, don't let me waver
If things get quite rough, which they may

I'll never give up on that boy
Nor will You for You promised him joy
For I know it was true, when he said "Yes" to You
Though the enemy seeks to destroy

I'll not quit as I intercede
For You are his Savior indeed
Though it may take years, I give you my fears
As I trust every moment I plead

And so in the gap I will stand
Heeding your every command
With help from above, I unconditionally love
And soon he will reach for your hand.

(Victorious Deliverance Ministries)

In July 2003 I was staying at Mom's for the Fourth of July and my class reunion. Elaine called me to ask for help getting Bill home. He was really drunk and friends kept calling her and trying to convince him to go home safely, but he refused to go. The next morning, she called to say she was ready to try an intervention to get Bill into treatment and asked for my help. It had been a bad night; she spent the whole night talking with her friend Kim, who encouraged her to give intervention a try. Her family had held an intervention for her and it led her to recovery. Mom and I agreed to provide the signatures of two family members required to force Bill to either enter treatment voluntarily or be committed. Mom thought Elaine should not sign the paperwork, which could make things more difficult between them in their marriage. I always admired Mom's decision and it made me think of her "standing in the gap for her son." We all met at Bill and Elaine's and my brother immediately knew something was up.

Many tears were shed. We told Bill how much we loved him and how concerned we were for his health and safety due to his alcoholism. We asked him to go to treatment and at the time he said he felt he had no other choice. Elaine's words to Bill were: "I can't stay married to you unless you get sober." He replied, "I can't stay married to you unless I am not!" What a battle. Their son Todd cried and said "I just don't want my family to break apart." Their oldest son Mark said "I don't want to take sides." I was praying for God to help us all.

I remember being hardly able to speak because I was crying so hard. I felt so weak; but not Mom, our team's most valuable player (MVP). She was leading us in prayer without an ounce of hesitation in her voice. She was simply amazing and I admired her enormous strength. One of the hardest things I had to do that day was play watchdog to my brother. He had to go outside to his work truck to get what he needed to complete his payroll. He said he had to get it done, so rather than let it be an excuse to put off checking into treatment, we needed to let him handle it. But we also needed to make sure he wouldn't just drive away. Kim told me: "Follow him out there Cathy, and make sure he doesn't leave." Fortunately he didn't try. He came back in, completed the work and went to the hospital to check in. Mom and I had to tell Nancy and Seth the results of the intervention. I had to explain to my husband why I couldn't come back home for another day as we tried to get the court order. Thank goodness he was supportive during this time. I hated being away from my kids, my husband and my home but I also felt it had to be done because I loved my brother and my family with all my heart. My other siblings were against this extreme measure for Bill's treatment and they wanted no part of our actions.

That night, Mom and I prayed together and I tearfully picked up the photo of her with the four of us—Nancy, Bill, Seth and Cathy—from her coffee table, wondering if another photo of its kind it would ever be taken again? Over the years so many wonderful, memorable times and similar poses had been photographed. A picture of a proud mother with her four children; however, they were always missing the father and husband. But to me, because of all Mom had done for us, it was a picture of pride and honor. Mom and I went to the courthouse the next day. When it came time to complete the paperwork, we had to voice how deeply concerned we were for Bill's health and safety. We had to state in writing that we felt he was a risk to himself or others, and if he was the court order would surely stand. It was one of the hardest things I have ever done in my life, but at the time I did believe it was the only way to save my brother. What I wrote in my statement was complete honesty and I believed treatment was absolutely necessary. Things became very strained between the other siblings and Mom and I because they were totally against our decision. Bill was furious with us because he had agreed to go to treatment. He didn't understand why we had to file the court order. We had been advised by Kim's family that it was the only way to force him to stay in treatment. Otherwise he could leave the program at any time.

Unfortunately, after a few agonizing days of heated phone calls among all of us, Mom and I agreed to withdraw the court order to save our family unit and our love and all we had shared throughout our lives together. I tried to explain why we did it in the first place to my sister and I wrote my brother Seth a note and left it on his car, to convince to speak to me about the situation. I wasn't sure Bill would ever speak to me again, but I thought if he stayed in treatment on his own and it worked, it would be worth it. However, that didn't happen and he was out within days. He did not stick to the outpatient protocol and his marriage remained in jeopardy. Kim's family was right; they knew by experience. Why didn't we listen to them? Bill didn't stay committed to treatment to try to save himself or his marriage, and I wondered if Mom and I had made a huge mistake by backing out of the court order. If my brother got hurt or died, or injured or killed someone, would I be able to live with myself? I prayed, I cried, I asked God to mend our family, to save my brother and to keep watching over all of us. I went home to my own family and life went on.

Our family relationships were rocky for about a year after, and I often wondered if we would ever be the way we were before the intervention. One thing was certainly clear: Bill's alcoholism was still negatively affecting his life, his marriage and his family members' lives. After Todd graduated from high school and a few months after their 25th wedding anniversary in 2005, Elaine decided to file for divorce. I was sad but I truly understood and had been expecting her painful decision. I hadn't lived it daily but I had seen, heard, felt and understood that it was her time to save herself. She had reached her breaking point. Some members of our family resented her for giving up on Bill, but I realized that wasn't it at all. Their marriage wasn't perfect; Elaine wasn't perfect and had faults as we all do. I believed there was no way to save their marriage if they didn't start breaking down the biggest barrier first—alcoholism. How many more marriages in our family would fail because of the ugly demon?

1 Corinthians 13:2

[2] If I have the gift of prophecy and can fathom all mysteries and all knowledge, and if I have a faith that can move mountains, but do not have love, I am nothing. (Biblica)

CHAPTER 3

Bases Loaded—A Familiar Pattern

When our lives are shattered we turn to whatever will get us through. No one can really question others' choices when they don't experience their anguish. I can't imagine the extreme amount of pain Mom must have felt and how totally alone she must have been years ago when she was left to raise four young children on her own. The pain and anger she must have had for my father had to be so deep, but she stayed in the game by being strong, optimistic, caring and always strong in her faith. Now I can relate personally to some of the financial and legal situations caused by Dad and his alcoholism that she had to overcome, not to mention her loneliness and the burden of being on her own. She has always had amazing strength and optimism, and I believe that most of it comes from her faith in God. The love I have for her will never leave me. Her example has influenced my life immensely. I love Dad too, but I don't feel the same kind of love for him; as a child I really couldn't love him because I didn't even know him. As an adult, I wanted to love him but he doesn't always make it easy to do.

Fortunately, Mom found love and happiness years later after her marriage and divorce from Dad. I understand now her need for that love, but I didn't at the time and I doubt that my siblings did either. She met and fell in love with Dean Carter, and they were married in 1976. He also had four children. I am the first to admit that the years with them in our family were some of the most difficult of my childhood. I resented my stepfather many days of my life. But Dean loved Mom every day and he did help provide for us. I will always be grateful for that and the years of happiness he gave to my mother. I often felt bad for Mom but at the same time admired her for how hard she worked and in a factory. My brother Seth and I both received college scholarships from her company, which were huge blessings for a poor family like ours.

A few years after Mom and Dean were married we sold our family home in Rock Falls and moved to Dean's family farm, 15 miles away near Clifton. Because I was still at home, I had to leave my childhood home, my friends, and my family community. It was particularly difficult because it was during my freshman year of high school. Living with the stepsiblings was a huge burden on me. One of my best friends, who lived across the street from us, and I even created the perfect solution and proposed it to Mom: I could stay in town and live with my friend and her family. Of course Mom didn't go for it and I was very upset at the time, but now I laugh when I think of it. Would she leave behind her baby? No way!

The hardest part of this move for me was losing my identity. I was no longer known as Nancy, Bill and Seth's the little sister in Rock Falls, in the community where our family was known (although some of our "celebrity" was negative due to Dad). I was now lonely in the country and a stepsister to Ted, Val, Keri and Robby. I had a hard time developing close relationships with any of my stepsiblings, particularly Keri or Robby, the ones closest to my age. Keri was mean and hurtful, and stole my clothes. Robby didn't have many friends and was treated as an outcast. I didn't know how to help him and find my own way too. My poor relationships with them left me resentful and depressed and I missed my old life terribly. I used my faith in God big time through the move and adjustment to a new home, a new high school and stepsiblings. I was blessed with new friends and found a way to be known not just as the stepsister new in Clifton. I remember writing a lot. My English teacher encouraged me to hang in there and keep journaling if it helped me get through the difficult time. I joined choir and accompanied the swing choir on piano. I dated and even had a high school sweetheart with a wonderful family. My high school years were blessed because I had many new friends and still kept the old ones. To this day, I am so grateful for many of the relationships I have because of that move to the farm/ Clifton. I am equally grateful for those back in my hometown of Rock Falls. A few people from each of those towns have been some of my closest, dearest, lifetime friends.

My stepfather was a good man and good to Mom, but he was also an alcoholic, which made him irresponsible in many aspects of his and our lives. In addition to farming, Dean drove a semi so he was frequently away. Mom continued to work her factory job, so a lot of the time I was alone with the stepsiblings and I hated it. In my years at home, my worst memory is a night that Dean wandered into my room and was passed out on the floor drunk. I couldn't figure out why he was acting this way, but he did eventually leave. Nothing bad ever happened, but I hated that night and it haunted me for a long time. I worried about him all the time. When I became an adult and moved away from the situation, I worried even more, especially for Mom, but she seemed so content. She loved him and their life together, especially being on the farm. I could see their devotion for one another, despite his drinking.

One decision I will always be happy with was the decision to have both Mom and Dean walk me down the aisle to give me away when I got married in 1988. I knew that Dad could not fulfill this role. He hadn't raised me and he really wasn't a father to me at all during my childhood. I was certain of one thing: Mom was going to give me away. She deserved the honor the most. I agreed to have Dean, too, because he was the closest thing I had to a father. There is a scene in our wedding video that is painful, but realistic. My husband and I, his parents, and Mom and Dean are preparing for the receiving line after the wedding. Dad is standing to the side dressed in his tuxedo watching us; eventually he steps out of the picture. It was like reality hitting him: he would not be included in this line. But when I asked myself why, the answer was very clear; he hadn't stepped up to the plate. He was not part of that line because of his choices and actions in life, his absence as a father, his alcoholism—reality.

Mom had a lumpectomy (which thankfully turned out fine). I went to stay with her and help her through it. I remember being so scared to leave her because Dean wasn't home and I knew where he was—the bar. I was so angry but Mom assured me she would be fine. How could you not be with your wife through something like that? How many alcoholic men was I going to have to deal with in my life? Why did this familiar pattern keep turning up in so many of the members of my family? Bases were loaded with alcoholics and I felt the only way to stay in the game was to rely on faith. So I kept praying.

My husband Jack and I started our lives together not far from both my hometowns and our first son, Ryan Jack was born in 1991. In November 1995 Grandpa Cane's health was failing and I was pregnant with my second son. Grandpa knew of Jacob Wayne's birth on November 7 and even told people who visited him in the hospital. It made me so happy that Grandpa knew about Jacob being born. A week later on November 14, Grandpa passed away and a little piece of all of us was gone. He loved his two daughters, he loved his three granddaughters, his three grandsons and all his great-grandchildren, and we all loved him just as much. The day after Grandpa's death, I called Mom from my home about 40 miles away and discovered that something was very wrong—she was slurring her words and not making any sense. I asked if Dean was home and she answered no. I told her I was calling for help. I immediately called my brother Bill in Rock Falls and told him that something was wrong with Mom and he had to go to the farm right away. He and Aunt Penny went there as fast as they could and found Mom lying on the kitchen floor. She'd had a stroke. She spent the next two weeks in the hospital in Rock

Falls. It was an incredibly emotional time for all of us, especially me, who had my newborn son, lost my grandpa and almost lost my mom. Thank God I called her when I did!

I have a few vivid memories from this time that I will never forget. My oldest son, Ryan, only four, had visited Grandpa with me all his life and made the sweetest gesture at the funeral home. He walked up to the casket and sang Grandpa a song. I think it was "You are my Sunshine." Aunt Penny and I stood there in tears clinging to one another. We will never ever forget it as long as we live. We always say he had a golden heart by doing this sweet little thing for his great grandpa. Another memory I have is being on the phone with my friend Pam, a coworker, before that call to Mom. Pam was the person I phoned back immediately to help me find Jack on the job and let him know that he needed to get home right away so we could get to the hospital to see Mom. I always thought it was ironic that she was the person who helped me that day. She too had been married to an alcoholic for years but had divorced him. Toward the end of this same tragic month for our family, Pam's former husband died in his 40s because of his alcoholism. I remember visiting Pam and her daughters and telling the girls at least they wouldn't live their lives always in fear wondering about their father's condition like I had. I felt incredibly sad for them to lose a parent to the *disease*. Their family tragedy didn't end there: just a few years ago Pam tragically died in an auto accident. My heart still aches for her daughters and her entire family and I would give anything to have her back.

I also remember when all of us were gathered at Bill and Elaine's home and Dad called. I assume he called because he must have heard of Grandpa's passing. I wouldn't speak to him. I remember angrily thinking "How could he call at a time like this?" I was so emotional and still so scared about the possibility of losing Mom and the last thing I wanted to deal with was my alcoholic father. Maybe I was cold and cruel but that was where my emotions were at the time.

I spent so much time at the hospital with Mom during her recovery that the hospital staff brought in a baby bed from the nursery for Baby Jacob. As Mom improved, she loved joking about this with her visitors. It was a good sign to see and maybe motivation for her to keep improving. Mom has the greatest love for all of her grandchildren.

Another detail I will never forget is who was waiting for us to arrive at the front door when we got to the hospital. My brother Bill—I fell into his arms and cried and cried because I was so scared we were going to lose Mom, too. But God had another plan. He wanted her to live a long, healthy life. She quit smoking and took better care of herself, and recovered from the stroke well. The timing of this unfortunate event caused many in our family to believe it was Grandpa's way of watching over Mom. As the saying goes, God works in mysterious ways.

On the day of the funeral my emotions were still running high. I remember sitting down in the church pew holding Jacob, preparing to say goodbye to my grandfather (we called his passing and Jacob's birth the circle of life). I was also aching for Mom's presence, but she wasn't there. She didn't get to attend her father's funeral because she was still hospitalized due to the stroke. I began to cry and was consoled by Seth's wife, Amy, sitting next to me. I think my husband even took Jacob from my arms. We all leaned on one another during this tragic time—our family full of love. My brother Seth delivered an amazing eulogy in which he named what trait each of us—his two daughters and six grandchildren—had received from Grandpa Cane. It was so beautiful and meaningful to all of us. He said Mom had her father's optimism and Aunt Penny, like her father, is a good friend. He said that my sister's success is her trait and that my brother Bill along with sharing a birthday with him, got wisdom from Grandpa. Seth said his gift was Grandpa's sense of humor, which he was clinging to at the time to get through the difficulty. Seth said that my trait from Grandpa was my honesty, and how Grandpa taught us not to put on any "airs." Seth went on to say our cousin Jeff inherited Grandpa's spirit, while his sister Anna received the gift of being popular. Seth said that even the night before the funeral her cousins couldn't get enough of Anna, and I thought of how happy that would have made Grandpa. I think the honesty I got from Grandpa is a huge part of who I am today and the kind of person I always want to be—true to myself and others—genuine.

Maybe because Grandpa was so much a part of all of us, he did have the power to help Mom make a miraculous recovery, for which I will always be thankful. Maybe it was all part of God's plan, or Grandpa's, or maybe the work of the two of them! Nevertheless, it did work and my Mom is healthy in her 70s and living an active life to this day. What a blessing! She has had an aortic aneurysm since 1999, but it has been monitored carefully and has not limited her lifestyle. She is blessed by her faith, church activities and many friendships in Rock Falls.

In summer 2002 I remember leaving the farm sick with worry about Dean—his health, lifestyle and what could happen when he drove home drunk from the bar night after night. I didn't understand how Mom could stay with him, but it was her choice and we each have to do what's best for ourselves. Dean had a severe cough that was painful to hear and I knew his years of drinking and smoking were starting to take their toll on him. I decided I had to give it to God so I prayed all the way home. I asked God to do what is best for Dean, for Mom and the future. I remember praying "I am turning this over to You, God, because I don't know what else to do." In early October, Dean passed out at home after a long day in the field. Mom tended to him until he was taken by ambulance to Rock Falls and died. Mom's heart was broken and I felt sick with the thought that this happened because of my prayer. But then I realized that only God had the answer, and the best thing was to end Dean's pain, which I think was greater than any of us realized. My siblings and I and our extended family were all there supporting Mom. She struggled for many months and even years after Dean's death, but she managed gracefully once again through faith, family and friends to find happiness after moving back to town from the farm. Mom missed farm life, the sunsets and memories she and Dean had made together and was very lonely, but her faith and resilience remained strong.

I admire Mom with the greatest pride. She has taught me so much in life, especially by her strength and her faith. Her guidance and love helped me grow up to become a responsible adult. Mom and I have always been close. Her example led me to my greatest joy in life—being a mother myself. All the years of love in my marriage to Jack and the birth of our three sons were truly blessings to me. We used Mom's maiden name and Grandpa's family name (Cane) when naming our third son: Sidney Cane Steele born in 1999. I loved my husband, our sons and our family life. But the longer we were married, the familiar pattern of alcoholism emerged in my husband and I wondered did I wind up in the same game? Were bases going to be loaded with my three sons on first, second and third and was it my turn to step up to the plate?

Hebrews 4:16

[16] Let us then approach God's throne of grace with confidence, so that we may receive mercy and find grace to help us in our time of need. (Biblica).

CHAPTER 4

Line Drives—Big Events

In most baseball games, line drives are a good thing, but many of them/big events in our family weren't so good. In January 2004, I remember coming home in the early afternoon as I was working part time then. My husband Jack had taken a call from my Aunt Rebecca saying that Dad had a heart attack. He required immediate surgery to put in stents to save his life. I called my sister and she and I made arrangements for our kids, our homes and our jobs, and left to see Dad together. Many times we've told one another that if we stick together, it will be easier, so it was our pact whenever we had to deal with Dad's chaotic life. He recovered, but his lifestyle was much the same. I never really understood how someone could go through that big of a scare and go right back to smoking and drinking. Dad lived most of his life with no real direction, no possessions—not even a car—to his name, living check to check, working odd jobs to get by.

What little money he had was spent on his addictions and playing pool. Most of his life, we didn't have an address or phone number to reach him. When he would come to visit us, we often had to drive to get him or he would take the bus, sometimes asking my sister for money to pay for his bus ticket. No matter what we did with our dad, we always seemed to pay the bill. It often made us feel like we were *his* parents. Many times we would make arrangements for Dad's visits and then at the last minute, he would call to say he couldn't make it. My sister and I had a phrase for this familiar pattern: "same story, different day." We wondered how many more years we would be living it.

A few years later in June 2007, Dad was found slumped over his desk at a telemarketing job he worked near his apartment. He was taken to the local hospital. That time my brother Bill was called first and he reached me at a basketball tournament to say Dad had a heart attack; it did not look good and we should come right away. My sister and I got in the car together again and took off. When we arrived Dad was on a ventilator and hooked up to many machines. He was surrounded by many of his drunken friends. After all it was the weekend! We didn't know them and their behavior was distressing to Dad, the medical team, and us, so we talked to the hospital staff and they were asked to leave. If I remember correctly, I think there was a little bit of a disagreement between his friend Jay and us when we tried to get Dad's apartment key from Jay. Dad let people stay with him for long periods of times even though it was against tenant rules. Both my brothers arrived that evening. We went to eat a meal and start planning Dad's funeral because the situation looked very grim. But to our surprise, Dad had a different plan and evidently God did too. Dad slowly starting making progress and a couple weeks later underwent open-heart surgery to repair the damage from the heart attack. During this same time, my sister's family lost a close friend suddenly after a fall from which he never recovered, and yes, his alcoholism was the cause of the accident. I didn't want my father to die but I kept wondering why he continued to be the lucky one. And did he realize it and would he try to change his life?

One of the most difficult tasks for my sister and me while Dad was still hospitalized and in bad shape was going to his apartment. Some of the mess actually made us sick but we worked together to do what we had to do. I remember hauling all his dirty laundry to be washed and back and trying to clean up his apartment, which was above a bar. We really had to push ourselves to deal with it all but somehow we managed. We had one another, we had our family and we had our faith. We even had our sense of humor: I remember joking that the next time, we were leaving it all to our brothers to handle! We were done! We discovered that he had been living without electricity. It was like a bad dream that our father actually lived this way. The electricity had been shut off because of unpaid bills. Before Dad left the hospital, I paid his electric bill with my credit card so he would have service again. He did pay me back, but much later. I am not sure whether or not he ever paid my sister back a single cent. I again questioned why he continued to live this way of life and when it would end.

Dad recovered amazingly well and over the next few years he sometimes went to his grandchildren's events and kept in touch with us on a regular basis. His lifestyle remained the same but as long as he could visit responsibly we allowed it. I am grateful that he had the opportunity to watch my sons' sports activities because I believe it meant a great deal to him. I think most of the athletic talent my sons have comes from my Dad. Sid has a particular fondness for Dad and during Sid's most imaginative childhood stage, my eldest son would joke that it is because both Sid and Dad live in a make-believe world! Dad loved to talk about his coaching days and I wondered if he ever wished he could relive the past. Hearing the same stories over and over again like he was stuck in the past was frustrating to us, but what else did he have to talk about? Life was good back then; he had it all. If only he hadn't let the alcoholism take over his life and cause so much destruction. We could have been such a wonderful family, all six of us together, happily ever after.

One of the hardest things to do when you love an alcoholic is trust them. They seem to find it easier to lie or just tell you what you want to hear than to tell the truth. I guess it makes sense in a way—maybe it's easier to lie when you live in a fantasy world and easier to tell the truth when you face reality. But do alcoholics realize what a line drive to our gut those lies are? I do not believe so or it wouldn't be so easy for them to keep doing it. How can you face truth, state truth, and live truth or reality when clouded by alcohol? It is not the fault of the alcoholic. The *disease* is to blame. We have to keep loving them and hating the *disease*. But it still makes us feel so many different emotions, as if we were riding on a roller coaster.

After Elaine divorced my brother Bill in 2006, he moved in with her brother Jerry Jens and continued to work his job and live his alcoholic lifestyle. The Jens and Nelson families were still close and we would have Thanksgiving dinners together until it wasn't fun to go to any more because of my brother's drinking. I didn't want my kids to see how bad it got and personally I didn't really want to see it either. I hated the example he was setting for our family and especially for our kids.

The next year Bill had an injured shoulder that required surgery. He eventually had surgery, went through physical therapy, and was healing and preparing to head back to work. Early one morning that July, Bill called me to tell me he had been in an accident with his work truck but he was fine. He said he wanted to tell me before I heard it somewhere else. He explained that he was trying to avoid a deer on his way to work early that morning and went into the ditch. I remember doubting his story at the time, but he was my brother and I loved him, so I told him so and that I was very glad he was safe. But I again wondered how many times he would he be so lucky?

The accident was Bill's second in a company vehicle and his employer had to take action because he was too much of a risk. His boss told him to get his shoulder taken care of and check into a treatment program, or walk away from his job of more than 30 years. They could no longer take the risk unless he was willing to step up to the plate, face his alcoholism and swing the bat himself. It was time for him to play the biggest game of his life. I had such high hope for him.

I remember the line drive to my gut shortly thereafter. Elaine's brother Jerry and I were talking about Bill's accident and he told me what really happened. Bill's accident was not on the way to work, it was on his way home from the bar in the middle of the night or should I say early morning? Bill had called Jerry to help him but before they could pull the truck from the ditch, someone had reported the accident so my brother was required to go to the hospital for testing. This news caused me to lose it emotionally and I cried and I screamed. I was so angry to think that he called all the people who love him that morning lying to them about the accident—even our dear mother! I contacted my sister and told her I needed to talk to her in person. When it came to my brother's alcoholism, she was finally starting to see the reality too and was worried about him. I had to tell her the truth in person. We sat and talked truthfully and asked ourselves why this kept happening to our family and then we cried and prayed.

We felt God had truly answered our prayers that fall when Bill decided to check into a 30-day treatment program out of state. This was not an overnight process; it took some time to make all of the arrangements and for him to make the commitment. My sister and I were very involved, which Bill didn't really like, but we knew he would not get there alone and we loved him and wanted to help him. We tried to keep in touch with Bill's sons. We encouraged them to take advantage of the opportunity to be there for their dad during his treatment.

My sister and I gave up a lot of time from our jobs, our husbands, and our children to assist in this process but we knew how truly important it was for his recovery. We were willing to take our turn at the plate, this time for our brother. Again our sister pact held, together this would be easier, just as it was with Dad. I remember that everything was still up in the air on the day Bill was supposed to leave for the treatment center, and I was begging God to make it happen. We had gotten too far to not move forward. Positive word came from the Bill's company last minute so my sister, our brother Bill and I went to Glendale for him to sign some paperwork before we took him to the out-of-state facility. The company was very family oriented and welcomed us with open arms. The entire time that we met with Bill's boss and his father, the office dog sat at Bill's feet. I thought it was an amazing site. It was as though the dog knew Bill was the one who needed extra love that day. "A good sign from God," I thought to myself. It had been a long haul but I was so proud of my brother and his HUGE step up to the plate—finally.

Despite our efforts at small talk, our trip in the car was pretty quiet. Stopping for lunch and sitting face to face was even harder. We eventually made it to our destination. The treatment center staff was absolutely wonderful to him and us. I can remember my sister and me both feeling such relief when we left that night. It was Bill's turn at the plate and God would be watching over him and our connected family field while the recovery game was played. I truly felt relieved that my brother was where he needed to be and finally safe.

Jerry phoned us on our way home and was pushing for Bill's things to be moved out of his house as soon as possible. We were so perturbed and asked for some time—we just got him to treatment that day! Only my sister and I truly understood the emotional roller coaster we had been riding, all the stress and burdens we were carrying, and all we were trying to do for others while balancing our own families and responsibilities. Every day of my life I thank God we had each other because I am not sure either of us could have done all we had to alone.

Bill's treatment counselor strongly recommended that he not return to the environment in which he had been living (near Rock Falls). Since Jerry wanted him to move out, we thought we had to move forward while he was in treatment, despite Bill's objection. I thought of the irony of Bill's alcoholism being connected to Rock Falls, just like my dad's. So there we were, a few weeks later, on a familiar field, but this time for a different player. We were packing up my brother's things and storing them until he could find a place to live and start his sober life. I loved the thought of that: a clean playing field and Bill starting over. I can even remember going to my church to thank God. I sat by my favorite stained glass window with Jesus in the garden, the spot I had prayed to so many times before about this dreaded *disease*, begging for answers, strength, and direction. But this time I was giving thanks and it was beautiful! I honestly don't know how people get through life without faith.

My brother completed the 30-day program. Mom and I attended a family session halfway through; he seemed down but appeared to be making an effort. His sons Mark and Todd visited him. When it was time for his release, my sister and I went to bring him home. He got settled in an apartment in Glendale and his employer sent him out of state to work. Being away from family and friends was difficult for him and led him to depression, but we all kept in touch and encouraged him to hang in there during those first months of sobriety. In 2008 just after Christmas, we celebrated his 50th birthday and I remember how much I enjoyed it being "alcohol free." Our family of love gathered and celebrating together, and for the first time in a long time no one was drinking! I wrote Bill a poem and put my heart and soul into my writing. I framed it for him and yes, it did address his recovery and how proud I was of the accomplishment. The following fall I also sent my brother a letter congratulating him on what I thought was his sobriety anniversary.

Our family took another line drive the next fall when we heard news of a Rock Falls family losing their youngest son/brother to alcoholism. We knew them well and it hit our family very hard. I remember thinking *how lucky* **our family** continued to be when it came to the *disease*. I remember copying the obituary and writing a note to my husband Jack. There I went again—begging a loved one to change his lifestyle. The night I gave it to him, he was downtown at a bar, so I left it in an envelope on his windshield. Another attempt by me to get someone else to change, and it wasn't working. Why didn't I get it? Why did I keep trying?

That November, Nancy called me at work one day to tell me Bill had lost his job because he broke his sobriety and violated the agreement he had with his company. She filled me in on the past six months for him including the fact that she feared he was suicidal. She had tried to handle it all on her own because she knew my marriage was beginning to fall apart. I think we all wondered that year if Bill was still sober. Was he hiding that he fell off the wagon? Why? My husband and I argued about it many times when I would urge him to quit drinking like my brother had. He would say to me: "He still drinks, Cathy." I never believed Jack, but then came another gut check. Bill had been honest with him, another alcoholic, but not to me, his sister for life. What a fool I had been, still trusting and believing in those alcoholics I loved. Each lie took another piece out of me emotionally. No one wanted to believe Bill gave up his sobriety and would risk his lifetime career after he had come so far. But now I believe he had been drinking most of the year. No one had the heart to tell me because they knew what my reaction would be. They were right. I became physically ill and had to leave work the day my sister told me. The answered prayer had only been temporary. I needed more coping skills for this insanity as I felt the line drive go right through me that time. This disease *alcoholism* was draining the life out of me and all I could think of is what a joke it must have been to my brother to receive my letter of congratulations on his continued sobriety. It was never discussed.

After this line drive, I felt that it was very important to talk with my nephews about their dad and his alcoholism. I was able to talk to Todd in person and I wrote a letter to Mark. I could tell Todd was very concerned about his dad and even feared he was suicidal. It broke my heart to see the next generation so deeply wounded by this *disease* plaguing our family. I openly told Todd he had to take responsibility for his own life, and Mark too. Their dad's safety was not their responsibility; he was a grown man. I tried to explain the "let go and let God" concept. They are amazing young men and I want them to rise above the *disease* and never let it take over their lives. I proudly I see them as the next generation off to a great start and I hope my sons are to follow.

Job 22:28

[28] What you decide on will be done, and light will shine on your ways. (Biblica).

CHAPTER 5

Hitting One Out of the Park—Facing Reality

Fall 2008 was difficult, and I was struggling in my 20-year marriage. Jack really crossed the line a few times. I was so tired of either going to bed alone every night or not being able to sleep because of my husband's drunkenness or him not being home. Some mornings I actually woke up feeling sick to my stomach from the smell when he was in bed with me. It's sad but true and although he always claimed to be working in the garage, which was his shop, I knew it was more about drinking while working late. Something was very wrong with this picture. Jack's own alcoholism had made our lives unmanageable. The years of refinancing mortgages to get by was no longer working. He was hardly home and rarely involved in our family life. His irresponsibility was becoming extreme, my trust was fading, and our debt was mounting. I was starting to have restless sleep worrying about our financial situation. For years I had begged him to drink less, work more, spend his free time with our family, live more responsibly, and work with me to improve our financial situation, but without success. Instead of waiting up and worrying about my teenager getting home safely, I was worrying about a middle-aged married man and father of three. I just couldn't tolerate some of the behavior any longer and feared the kids were being negatively affected. We argued frequently or just simply avoided each other, but fortunately the anger never became physical. I can remember him getting so angry with me one morning that winter that he hit the wall and broke the light switch in our bathroom. I know it was the alcohol, often his foul mood was due to that. I walked by the cracked switch daily and it made me so angry every time. Where had the man I fell in love with gone and how could I get him back?

That same fall Jack asked me if I minded him being the driver for a female friend's bachelorette party. He spent bar time with her and other women often which was very upsetting to me. I said I didn't approve of the party idea, but he did it anyway. I was appalled at his decision and wondered if he would approve of me doing the same for a group of men. One Saturday he was acting very strange while getting ready for a football game. I finally figured out that he had been up all night drinking and was going to keep drinking through the football game. After the game he came back and actually passed out in the daylight on our patio. I was so afraid our oldest son and his friends would come by and see it, not to mention our younger kids at home. I finally got him to go to bed at 6:00 pm. I cried the rest of the night trying to figure out what to do. All I ever wanted was for my husband to love our family and me, to be by my side raising our kids together. None of his behavior seemed right and wasn't setting a good example for our sons. My effort to do it all and to cover up for him to our kids and so many others was really taking its toll on me. I hated the lie that our lives had become. In reality there was not much left of our marriage and I had already probably stayed in it too long.

For the first time that October, on our oldest son's birthday, I woke up and read my *Daily Word* and decided the time had come to face reality and tell my husband for the first time, that if nothing changed, our marriage would end. This was Step 1 of my 12-step program: "We admitted we were powerless over alcohol—that our lives had become unmanageable." *Daily Word* had been a symbolic devotional for our family for years and we often felt bonded by its messages. I had never mentioned separation or divorce to Jack before. I think I lived in denial for years because we were making it and I didn't want to face reality. I wanted to keep our family together (just like my nephew Todd did with his family years before), but I was also burned out by the disease of alcoholism and didn't want history to repeat itself. I was already the daughter of an alcoholic, the stepdaughter of an alcoholic, and the sister of an alcoholic. How could this possibly be happening to me again? Now I was the wife of an alcoholic! For years, I had prayed so many times about this problem, but I knew by the *Daily Word* message that day that it was time to face reality. October 15, 2008: "I am upheld and strengthened by the grace of God throughout times of dealing with both everyday matters and major difficulties. I rise up and move forward, supported fully by the grace of God" (*Daily Word* 2008). This was Step 2 of my 12-Step program: "Came to believe that a Power greater than ourselves could restore us to sanity." My belief that my brother Bill was sober created space within myself to face reality in my own family. I began to live out these words and the steps of the Al-Anon program. I taped up Bible verses at home and work, left them on my nightstand, and even carried them in my pocket some days. My favorite verse is Proverbs 3:5-6. This verse became my way of life and I referred to it often.

⁵ Trust in the LORD with all your heart and
lean not on your own understanding;
⁶ in all your ways submit to him,
and he will make your paths straight.[a] (Biblica).

Another incident occurred that winter when Jack's cell phone provider called to inform us that Jack's phone and leather jacket were turned in at their store. My 13-year old took the call which upset me. When I picked up the items, I checked the phone and found a voicemail from a woman. Jack also left a voicemail when trying to track down the phone. In the message, he told the woman not to call back, as if he were covering up the fact that she had the phone. The pit in my stomach felt as big as a baseball and I had to find a way to end the madness. When I confronted Jack with this he said it was just the bartender making sure he got home safely. Whether that was the truth or not, I guess he was more concerned that the bartender knew about his safety than that his wife of 20 years knew. It made my anger and hurt even greater.

By that Christmas I had reached my own point of insanity. It took my 17-year-old son to point it out to me. We had a fight—which was a rare occurrence in our great, mother-son relationship. He said, "Mom, you are taking your problems out on me." I had been so emotional and what we were fighting over wasn't the real issue. Suddenly it hit me, another line drive. Ryan was right, this way of life, alcoholism in our home, had driven ME to insanity and as a mother of three amazing sons, I couldn't let it go on. It was then I decided I would not live another year like the last and began to take action. My number one role in life was to be the best mother I could and that role was now in jeopardy. I owed it to my kids to find a way to maintain a happy home and care for them to my best ability, but I needed help. My closest friends, Jo and Michele, who had already been with me through so much, encouraged me to go my husband's family first, so I did. I contacted Jack's sister Bonnie and she told me that at Thanksgiving she had sensed there were problems by how Jack was treating me. She told me that others in the family had noticed too, but no one knew how to approach me. I felt so relieved to hear this. I hadn't lost my mind, others could see it, and a huge weight was lifted. I told our oldest sons, ages 17 and 13, about my plans. My oldest said, "Mom, you can't ask Dad to quit drinking, that is who he is." I will never forget that as long as I live. My son was becoming a young man and his perception of what was happening was incredible, but how sad it was that he had this view of his father. I truly felt I had to step up to the plate and show these boys a more responsible way of life in their most impressionable years. I was scared to death and not sure how I would ever pull it off financially. Thank God my two best friends were there to hold me together.

A few weeks later Bonnie, another sister-in-law Mary and I had a spontaneous intervention with my husband to try to convince him that things had to change. It went better than I expected; he agreed to see his doctor and try to make changes in his lifestyle. He said he didn't want our marriage to end and that he hadn't put in all these years to just walk away. I was so relieved—I wasn't sure what he would do, but he didn't leave and I thought we still had a chance. I kept praying and trusting in the Lord.

For about one month, Jack saw his doctor and started taking an antidepressant. Things did improve. He spent more time with us, less time going out, less drinking and less spending money. It was a good month; the kids could see the difference in him, and I tried to show my love and support. But into the second month, he gradually slipped back into the old habits. The lies and excuses were back and the drinking and time away from home increased. The irresponsible behavior returned, which led me on March 1 to give him an ultimatum: "You have two weeks to decide if you are going to face your addiction and make changes, or move out." Neither one of us wanted to ruin Ryan's run at the state basketball tournament going on at the time. Two weeks later he told me he thought separation was for the best and I agreed. I remember the day before he told me his decision, his friend Tim called early in the morning. I woke him to take the call but later that day he mentioned a message on his cell phone from the same person. I asked him if he remembered speaking to his friend that morning. But he didn't. The next day he said that he knew by the look on my face that I had reached the end of my rope and he had to leave. When we told our kids of our plans to separate, our 9-year-old said, "Dad, I really don't think it will be that different, you aren't home that much anyway." Once again I observed our kids' acute perception, this time from our youngest child. If a 9-year-old could see reality, why couldn't his dad? It made me feel so sad yet so assured I was doing the right thing.

The next few days and months were some of the most difficult in my life. Some days I was so depressed that I could hardly function. I gradually called closest family and friends to tell them about our separation, but could only make a couple of calls per day because of the overwhelming toll it took on me. I leaned heavily on friends Jo and Michele and my dear next-door neighbors, Dale & Millie, who had been family friends to us for years. Two days after Jack left I had a complete meltdown after leaving work for an appointment. I didn't know what to do so I drove to my church and sat by my favorite stained glass window of Jesus in the garden. I cried and I prayed to God for strength. Then I went to the church office. The secretary took one look at me and asked if I needed help. She hugged me until the minister came to meet with me. As I sat and told my story, his eyes often filled with tears. He was the father of three sons too and I know he was hurting for all of us. He prayed with me, gave me suggestions on how to help the boys and myself. It was a start and I am glad my melt down led me there. God carried me out and helped me on my way. Closest friends of my sons and their families were also incredibly supportive to the boys and to me.

Every day was hard but I had also found some peace. I was reminded why I wanted the separation: because I couldn't live the way we were any longer. As the boys and I left the house every morning, I felt peace, not anger and resentment toward my husband because he still wasn't home or out of bed. Before the separation I would go home for lunch and find him still sleeping off the night before. That angered me so much because our debt was mounting, and he wasn't even trying to work hard to remedy the situation. By his absence in the separation, we were now on a new God-guided path. I read it daily in devotions and felt it daily in the deep love for my sons and our lives together. The serenity was beginning and I found it in the prayer known to many: "God grant me the serenity to accept the things I cannot change; courage to change the things I can; and wisdom to know the difference." (*The Serenity Prayer*, <u>One Day at a Time in Al-Anon</u>)

It was interesting to see what people in our lives had seen our separation coming or those who were shocked by it. Most people were not surprised, which made me wonder how long I had been fading. Others must have seen it too, but thank goodness Ryan had the strength to tell me. His golden heart came shining through in that amazing act. You really learn who your friends are by those who reach out to you during separation and divorce. However, for as many people who were there for the kids and me, there seemed to be just as many who just walked right by, ignoring our family's deep pain, including adults who were supposed to be role models to our growing kids.

After more encouragement from dear friends, I went to my family doctor for help and sought counseling through my employer. I was diagnosed with "anxiety and depression due to situational stress." Alcoholism was once again sucking the life out of a family member—me, while the alcoholic—my husband—partied on. I realize that I would not have recovered so well emotionally if it were not for these professionals. By late spring, I was coping and the kids and I adjusting, but with little contact with Jack. He basically checked out of our family. The behavior and distrust disgusted and hurt me so deeply. "How could he want his life as an alcoholic more than life with a loving family?" There they were again: those same questions I had asked of my dad, my stepdad and my brother. I considered the support group for family members of alcoholics known as Al-Anon but didn't try it until months later. I began to realize once again with this alcoholic man in my life, the problem was the *disease*, not him. It made me still hate the *disease* with a passion! Mom gave me some of her Al-Anon books and as I added the daily readings to those from my *Daily Word*, I learned my life was no different than so many others in the program. Those words helped me escape my insanity on many days. It was all I could do to take care of the kids and home and handle my job every day without losing it.

My husband and I tried counseling together late spring; those sessions were extremely difficult. Jack didn't want to be there, but I told myself I couldn't give up on us unless we tried. One appointment was early in the morning, typically not a good time of day for him and it showed when he arrived late to our session and was irritable. At one session the counselor asked Jack if he was willing to give up alcohol in order to save our marriage. His answer was no. So many times his actions had already told me the answer but to hear it aloud was very painful. Jack thought the counselor was worthless and didn't like anything he had to say. I think that no matter what counselor we used, it wasn't going to work. He didn't want to step up to the plate.

The boys had their tough times and I tried to stay strong for them. In the beginning, I think my oldest had the hardest time, probably because he perceived how it would end and was already facing reality himself. My middle son was quiet in the beginning but occasionally expressed his emotions, which I always encouraged. Friends would often tell Jacob that they had seen his dad's work van at a local pizza shop. But Jacob would tell them that his dad wasn't out for pizza, he was at the bar next door. I hated that bar and the people who continued to serve Jack and spend time with him when they knew where he should have been—*with his family*. I was proud of the honesty in my teenage sons. The changes in our lives had matured both of them. I continued to believe that "facing reality" (which led to separation and divorce) was the right decision, not just for me but for them too. I think they understood and were learning so much about the men they wanted to become. My youngest son still wanted the fairy tale—his mom and dad happily ever after—and he had some rough patches. Sid savored any time he had with his dad as any young child would. I continued to sense his comfort level safe within our family home and he often melted my heart by pouring out his love toward me! I set up support at school for him. His teacher, the counselors and the staff were wonderful to Sid. I encouraged Jack to work on the relationships with each of our sons. I didn't have high expectations, and braced myself for the realization that he may be incapable of having healthy relationships without ever facing his alcoholism. I understood but still thought about how terribly unfair it was. I know how much we all loved one another. Unfortunately, an alcoholic's actions often bring more hurt than love. In order to understand this, I had to teach my children what I had already learned too many times before: it is not the people we love, but the *disease* affecting them.

Months after counseling with my husband, I tried Al-Anon but I wasn't ready. I would sit and cry and not speak, so I didn't go back again for a while. I filed for divorce in August 2009. That fall my doctor, counselor and friends kept encouraging me to try Al-Anon, so I went back. Once I got into the habit of going weekly, it was so good to have that hour listening to others talk of the same insanity I had lived, but also the hope for learning ways to find serenity for ourselves. I was no longer fighting reality, but accepting it. I was not waiting for my husband to change, but realized that I could change for me!

I remember trying to have a few conversations with Jack about my depression during our separation and through the divorce. It was odd to me that he tried to blame some of the issues we struggled to resolve on my depression. I could never convince him that his alcoholism drove me to my condition. I continued to work the other steps of Al-Anon program and take advantage of the resources available to me for my recovery. I know in my heart that by "facing reality" in one of the most difficult years of my life, I am truly the lucky one. I am still doing what I wanted to most in my life every single day: being a mother and raising my family. Even with all the uncertainty, that simple fact, my sons' love and God's strength are what keep me going.

I love the saying "Home is where the heart is." The timing of the changes in my family's lives were in part due to my sons and their strengths: the youngest with his realism on how little time his dad spent at home, the middle with his quiet understanding of the bigger picture—where his father was spending the time and the oldest with his maturity in helping me realize how truly weak I had become and that I had to save myself. There was a reason God put these big strong young men in my life. My weakness made me receptive to feed on their strengths. The next summer we sold our family home of 14 years and moved down the street to a rental. The buyer, timing of the sale, the relief of the financial burden and finding our new home in the neighborhood were truly the work of God, I was sure of it. It was hard to give up the house, our beautiful yard, our home where I rocked my babies, where they ran and jumped and played and where they grew. In that home we had so many wonderful years of happiness and memories and raising our sons, but I knew our marriage had reached the point of no return. I also didn't want the boys to think that our married life was what it should be, or for them to think that our financial situation was typical of adults in their 40s. I could no longer be happy in the house, knowing how dire our financial situation had become. I remember how proud I was the day I fixed that light switch Jack had broken. The insanity within those walls of our family home had come to an end. Positive changes were starting to take place. I was starting to find a way to fix things that were broken, including my heart.

Toward the end of our marriage I became frustrated with Jack's lack of motivation and inability to follow through with his responsibilities. Jack being his own boss as a self-employed contractor was not a good thing when coupled with alcoholism. My frustration with his irresponsiblity lingered during the divorce process too. It has to be a trait of an alcoholic, putting things off and not following through. I worked so hard trying to sort out all of the business, financial, housing, legal and tax matters through the divorce while he would drag his feet or not agree to most of it. We were only rendered a final agreement after we were forced into mediation. However, instead of signing off right away he dragged it out longer. It really took the cake to me when he insisted on more of my retirement money for the months he had waited by not signing the agreement. At the time I just wanted to move forward, not back, so went with my attorney's advice and agreed. Thank goodness I was in counseling at the time, because working through my anger at his nerve took a lot of effort.

I regretted that the divorce happened during Ryan's senior year, but friends told me that there never is a good time to get a divorce. I also had to remember what an impressionable time of their lives it was and to remember how important positive influence would be for them. That summer as Jacob, Sid and I were trying to settle into our new place Ryan admitted he truly felt displaced. It broke my heart, but I also knew he was starting out on his own new adventure in college and I told him that I hoped he would always consider wherever I was to be his home. When he comes home to visit now, I can tell clearly he does and what a relief that is to me. Many people told me a house is just rooms and walls; what matters are the people inside and their well-being. I have to remember that everything I miss isn't gone. It is tucked away in little pieces of my heart, my treasures. Home IS wherever your heart IS, forever, as long as you keep the memories close to your heart.

Matthew 6:21

[21] For where your treasure is, there your heart will be also. (Biblica).

Proverbs 3:5-6

[5] Trust in the LORD with all your heart and lean not on your own understanding;
[6] in all your ways submit to him, and he will make your paths straight.
[a] (Biblica).

CHAPTER 6

Pinch Runners—Where to Turn

When you begin a challenging journey, it helps to know you are not alone. You need to know that God and special people in your life are with you. I know that all my pinch runners were with me during the game and even stepped in for me many days, giving me the courage and strength I needed. I had several difficult years through separation and divorce, but I can always say I made it because of my faith, family and friends.

In baseball, a pinch runner is "a player substituted for the specific purpose of replacing a player on base. In the typical case, the pinch runner is faster or otherwise more skilled at base-running than the player for whom the pinch runner has been substituted" (Wikipedia). During the toughest times of my separation and divorce, I definitely had some pinch runners sub in for me. If they hadn't, I am not sure I would have known where to turn or whether to go toward first base or third. One really important thing I learned is: it's OK to ask for help and even if you don't, amazing people see you need it and reach out to you and help you accept their support. First and foremost in this role was God. As I have always known, He is the constant in my life. His messages came to me through our family favorite, *Daily Word*, as well as The *Bible* and the Al-Anon books. Sometimes the daily message and my faith were the only things that got me through the day! This was Step 3 of my 12-step program: "Made a decision to turn our will and our lives over to the care of God *as we understood Him.*"

My best friends Jo and Michele were the biggest MVPs of the game and were with me every step of the way, from listening to my cries of desperation any hour of the day, my fear and hurt, to helping me know how and where to turn, to actually getting through each day with the best outcome possible in the end. The thanks I owe them can never fully be repaid and the lifetime friendships I have with them are priceless. So many friends were there for me, the boys, and our family and not only pinch ran, but cleaned up the field inning after inning. They all worked so hard helping us to have a wonderful graduation for Ryan and, a couple of months later, to move. The Nelsons had already been through the hassles of broken families too many times, so I was grateful to have friends with me every step of the way. Michele would talk to me any hour of the day and sent me courage after counseling when I would have to compose myself and return to work. She also was huge in supporting me on the difficult day I filed for divorce. Jo was a huge help in the financial decisions and always lent a supportive ear. Their friendships were sisterhood for me. I knew we were in them for life.

Many other friends were there for me and gave me with advice from their own experiences of alcoholism or divorce. They passed on resources and did things for my kids that truly made a difference during the most difficult months. Many friends, including men who are dads for whom I have the utmost respect, showed their concern, support and generosity. It meant more than they will ever know. I have such admiration for many men who go beyond, stepping up to the plate for their families. People didn't realize it, but there were so many times I just sat in the car and cried while waiting to pick the kids up from events. I didn't have the strength to face people because I was hurting so badly. Shortly after the separation, at a sporting event, a longtime friend looked across Sid at me and asked how I was doing. I couldn't even respond, so he just held out his hand and I placed mine in his. He just held it there for a few minutes, out there in public. It didn't matter, he knew I needed someone to reach out to me and he took his turn. Support such as this, favors for my kids and extra money being thrown here and there were huge during this very difficult time. I remember having lunch with my friend Melanie one day and sharing all my pain, and how surprisingly our laughter came too. It led us to the thought of me writing a book about all I had endured. The title, *Stepping Up to the Plate*, was her idea! Thanks, Mel! Here we go, girlfriend!

I also found peace at a place where I often went to walk and pray. It is a special park in town with a big pond, beauty and nature (my cover photo). It was a place for connecting with God and releasing my emotions. It was a place where I made big decisions and evaluated where I had gone wrong and how I could move on. I chose to tell my sons my plans to file for divorce at this location. I shed so many sad tears there, but later could go and find it so peaceful and uplifting. It was part of my healing and my serenity. This was Step 4 of my 12-step program: "Made a searching and fearless moral inventory of ourselves."

My employer also played a big role by provided an "Employee Assistance Program" that directed me to the counseling I so desperately needed. One of the most important things that counseling taught me is something I share with others whenever possible: Don't drive yourself crazy trying to find **reason** in the behavior of an alcoholic; you never will. Wow—it seemed so simple once I heard it then, but I had been trying my entire life. I was trying to figure out why their behavior didn't make sense to me. Dad's lifetime addiction and lack of life direction, my stepfather's lifestyle, my brother's years of ups and downs, and finally, my husband's daily alcoholism resulted in me reaching a level of insanity I could no longer take. At Jack's intervention, my sister-in-law Bonnie said it best when she told her brother, "Jack, your wife is drowning." In counseling I also learned how to only put on my plate what was absolutely necessary each day. I learned to not try to figure out my life plan and to simply focus on a few critical things I had to deal with that day. I also learned to not expect so much from myself; I was doing the best I could, and trust in the Lord was key.

My counselor was incredibly wise and helped me through my suspicions that Jack might have been unfaithful to me. But when I considered the alcoholism, the financial situation and the fact that he didn't want to spend time with me or the kids, infidelity was just one more thing to add to the list of why I had no choice but to go through with the divorce. I still don't know the absolute truth and it is very hard to think he may have been unfaithful. After all, alcoholics and honesty don't typically go hand in hand. I had to let go of how he had let me down, which was especially hard when it came to the kids. My counselor kept reinforcing the idea of no expectations. If you don't have expectations, you won't be disappointed, but I still thought it was unfair. In marriage and life, I believed that meeting expectations mattered. I believe that I had put into our marriage what I vowed I would. Why couldn't he?

My family doctor was incredible. He prescribed medication to help me work through depression and anxiety brought on by my circumstances. At first, he would have me come in often to monitor how well or not so well I was doing, making sure I was taking care of myself. I appreciated him so much. No one was more proud than him of my progress. I value what he as a caring professional did for my recovery. This year at my physical I told him I was concerned about gaining weight and he told me it was all right, it meant I was happy again. He had truly witnessed my transformation.

People in your support group are like your teammates because they understand what you are going through and they tell you it is OK to cry, laugh, or be angry. I will always be a person who believes in and supports Al-Anon. I admit it is not easy to go in the beginning or even to find the right group, but even just the literature is so valuable and makes complete sense when you are struggling through the worst of times. My youngest son also attended a support group for almost a year, and the unique aspect of it was that he didn't even realize it was therapy because they played games that worked on building self-esteem. The staff, counselor and teachers at the local elementary school that all our boys attended were amazingly supportive to Sid also.

Almost a year after the divorce was final, I was able to attend a Christian workshop for divorcées based on the Bible verse Jeremiah 29: 11-14.

Jeremiah 29:11-14

[11] "For I know the plans I have for you," declares the LORD, "plans to prosper you and not to harm you, plans to give you hope and a future. [12] Then you will call on me and come and pray to me, and I will listen to you. [13] You will seek me and find me when you seek me with all your heart. [14] I will be found by you," declares the LORD, "and will bring you back from captivity.[a] I will gather you from all the nations and places where I have banished you," declares the LORD, "and will bring you back to the place from which I carried you into exile." (Biblica)

It was at this workshop where I was able to share with others in similar situations some of the most difficult experiences I had endured. It felt good to keep healing and learning from others but also have something to give back. One of my favorite things from this workshop was Sister Mary's comment: "We all started in the heart of God and we go back there often." She encouraged us to remember what God feels like, and I also loved that idea. We were asked to describe how we had experienced God's faithfulness to us as individuals. This was easy for me because I had overcome so many obstacles in my childhood and adult life (many related to alcoholism) but somehow remained strong enough to survive. I believe it was all because of God's faithfulness to me. Each time His presence helped me, not only to work through the heartache, but also to gain strength to move on. During the workshop, we discussed how each phase you go through in divorce is important, admitting your mistakes, realizing where you are along the way, and honoring the feelings as you experience them because they wouldn't always be there. It made me think of us as players having our own speed around the bases in the game and having those pinch runners step in for us from time to time, when they were more capable. This was Step 5 of my 12-step program: "Admitted to God, to ourselves, and to another human being the exact nature of our wrongs."

Sister Mary reminded us that "God is a God that won't go away." How incredibly true that is. He hasn't left me my whole life through every challenge, through each alcoholic man in my life, and through the many divorces in our family, most definitely my own. We were encouraged to think about God's story of hope for us, His best dream for us, and our best dream for ourselves. We were asked to think about what might be holding us back from this dream, what it would take to achieve it, and how we would embrace all that became new. We were asked to proclaim what God has done for us and bring into view what we couldn't see, and to think about what we wanted to do to bring ourselves into the light. I believe my divorce forced me to proclaim what God has done for me by bringing into view the reality of my life. He showed me what I had to do to restore myself and persevere in order to raise my sons responsibly. To bring myself into the light, I want to help those I love and other families affected by alcoholism. I want something good to come from all I have been through and I hope I am doing so by sharing my experiences and improving my character. I hope my words will be a guide toward faith, which will in turn help others step up to the plate and make it safely home, wherever that may be for them, for each to find their own way to survive and heal. This was Step 6 of my 12-step program: "Were entirely ready to have God remove all these defects of character."

You always assume you have your family members backing you in life and if you are lucky, you do. I know it was hard for Mom to see me in pain and I hated for her to worry, but knowing she was praying constantly was all I needed from her. She also was a good listener when I did confide in her. I really didn't turn to my brothers. While I am sure they were concerned, they didn't really offer much support. In the beginning my sister seemed agitated that I would even consider separation and divorce. She would send me articles about commitment and working things out. She didn't see that just like in my brother's marriage, the biggest barrier in mine was alcoholism and until we addressed that, our chances did not look good. I appreciated what Nancy was suggesting but it takes two people for those methods to work and she had no idea how far gone our marriage was and how financially buried we were. There were times when I felt like Jack's sisters understood more than my own. It wasn't that she didn't want to understand or to care—she simply was burned out because the *disease* of alcoholism, which ran through generations in our family, was taking the life out of her too. She just wanted to love and enjoy her own family for once and give them her all. Who can blame her? This *disease* had been an ugly part of all of our lives for entirely too long.

I have always had a deep connection with Mom's only sister, Penny, even though she lives far away. We are a lot alike and I honestly believe she understands me better than anyone I know. She was also a pinch runner and one who especially helped me see the strength of my faith and how to use it to help myself. I am very thankful for all of my family. My kids were amazing at different times. They would give me the lifts I needed, and I am just so happy to still have them with me every single day. My husband's family was in a difficult place, but they never made me feel that way. They understood that their brother was ill and that I had done all I possibly could. They knew that I was raising the boys on my own for the most part and they kept me in the family because they wanted, as I did, the kids to still have their aunts, uncles and cousins. I even had to remind my own family that you don't just shut people out, like they had done to my former sister-in-law, Elaine at times. Even after divorce, there will always be ties because of the kids. The oldest Steele sister, Doris, even said, "Cathy divorced our brother, not us." I will never forget that as long as I live. Often sister Bonnie asked me, "What is left in the marriage for you?" My answer was not much. I never dreamed I would be in the position to walk away from my 21-year marriage, but I worked through mistakes I had made and God guided me to knowing it was the right decision. The support I felt was huge and I value everyone who helped me get through. Thanks, pinch runners! I am so glad I knew where to turn. This was Step 7 of my 12-step program: "Humbly asked Him to remove our shortcomings."

[15] **Genesis 28:15**

[15] I am with you and will watch over you wherever you go, and I will bring you back to this land. I will not leave you until I have done what I have promised you." (Biblica).

CHAPTER 7

7th Inning Stretch—Same Story, Different Day

We have reached that point of the game where we stand up, stretch and take a break. It's time for a deep breath, reflection on the enjoyment of the game and gazing at the beauty of the field. In my life it is the point at which I am able to pause, thank God for all I have and feel His presence, which reassures me I cannot change other people, only myself. It's time to forgive those who hurt me and make amends for my own mistakes. After reaching middle age and dealing with generations of alcoholism in my family, I understand that it is going to be the same story **every day** no matter what I do. I think my sister finally does too after all we have been through. We are still saying to one another when it comes to alcoholism in our family: "same story, different day." Her realization has helped mend our relationship, which I know I will have for my lifetime and that is a great blessing to me. Relationships with alcoholics are not dependable, but as sisters and all we have endured, we still know what we always have—that we have each other. We have our pact, have kept it, and it will get us through anything in the game. This was Step 8 of my 12-step program: "Made a list of all persons we had harmed, and became willing to make amends to them all."

Although difficult to comprehend, the truth is that it doesn't matter what you or anyone else does to try to help the alcoholic, they keep doing what they want to do, including taking advantage of us. I believe that is the lesson to learn: we each have to do what is best **for ourselves** no matter how much love we have for others. No matter how much it hurts to see the destruction, the alcoholic has chosen that way of life. We chose to cope. It really is the same story, different day, but how do we want to live it and shouldn't we live for ourselves?

A daily devotion that I came across explains how we should live, by accepting Jesus into our hearts and giving our lives to him.

Come to Me . . . Matthew 11:28-30— "Come to me, all you who are weary and burdened, and I will give you rest. Take my yoke upon you and learn from me, for I am gentle and humble in heart, and you will find rest for your souls. For my yoke is easy and my burden is light."

"Isn't it humiliating to be told that we must come to Jesus! Think of the things about which we will not come to Jesus Christ. If you want to know how real you are, test yourself by these words—'Come to Me . . .' In every dimension in which you are not real, you will argue or evade the issue altogether rather than come; you will go through sorrow rather than come; and you will do anything rather than come the last lap of the race of seemingly unspeakable foolishness and say, 'Just as I am, I come.' As long as you have even the least bit of spiritual disrespect, it will always reveal itself in the fact that you are expecting God to tell you to do something very big, and yet all He is telling you to do is to 'Come . . . Come to Me . . .' When you hear those words, you will know that something must happen in you before you can come. The Holy Spirit will show you what you have to do, and it will involve anything that will uproot whatever is preventing you from getting through to Jesus. And you will never get any further until you are willing to do that very thing. The Holy Spirit will search out that one immovable stronghold within you, but He cannot budge it unless you are willing to let Him do so. How often have you come to God with your requests and gone away thinking, 'I've really received what I wanted this time!' And yet you go away with nothing, while all the time God has stood with His hands outstretched not only to take you but also for you to take Him. Just think of the invincible, unconquerable, and untiring patience of Jesus, who lovingly says, 'Come to Me' . . ."

My Utmost for His Highest. (2010).
Website: www.utmost.org

When I first ready this devotion, all I could think about were the people in my life for whom I have been praying to "Come to Jesus," wishing they had the courage to step up to the plate or to cross the line, or just accept Jesus and the rest would follow—a new way of life in sobriety. It sounds simple, but I know addiction is powerful and it can take hold of a person for years or even a lifetime. I have seen it firsthand for generations. I wanted to share the piece with all of them but would it just be like all the other pleas or messages I have passed on to them? "The Holy Spirit will search out that one immovable stronghold within you, but He cannot budge it unless you are willing to let Him do so"—that is, the individual, not his family or friends, has to UPROOT whatever is preventing him from getting to Jesus.

I think that is one of the hardest things for the family members or friends of an alcoholic to understand. How can alcohol be more important than a marriage, family, friendship, job, financial security, or faith? How can alcoholics want to be controlled by the *disease* when people who love them are willing and are there for them and God has his arms outstretched waiting for them to *Come*? I look at it as the addiction having such a tight hold on alcoholics that they can't break free to find what is in them, what reality is, or who Jesus is, until they totally accept Him and the power of what He can do. Alcoholism allows addicts to stay in a fantasy world—evading responsibility, staying sad, and living an unmanageable life because they think it is easier and less painful. Perhaps it is less painful for them or the alcohol numbs the pain, so they keep drinking. But not for those of us who watch them let it destroy so much, along with pieces of ourselves. Why can't they see the beauty of our Lord? He is ready for us to come any time. He would show them the way.

There is no way I would have ever made it through my life without coming to Him and resting in His strong arms from time to time, especially during my separation and divorce. My Bible study described those who want this from God, clinging to His legs like our kids did when they were young. As mothers, my friend and I studying the lesson loved this! God is waiting to pull us in whether we take a simple step forward or we grab hold of Him and cling tightly. The hard part is that movement to do so, simply . . . *Come to Him.*

My eyes well with tears at the beautiful thought of God with his hands outstretched to take in my dad, my stepdad (now deceased), my brother Bill, the father of my children and friends with the *disease*. I think they have all felt God's presence or his arms reaching out to them, and many of them have taken a step or two toward Him but not all the way up to the plate. Bill actually did and made it home during his treatment year, but was called out at the plate by letting the *disease* consume him once again. I will continue to pray that one day all of them simply *Come*.

Nancy counted up how many times she had moved Dad in the last ten years because of his chaotic lifestyle of alcoholism—more than a handful for sure. A few years ago she thought we had found the perfect solution in his last move to a reduced-income apartment near a grocery store and a senior citizens center. All his needs were in one place and farther from the bars. This type of arrangement seemed manageable and made sense to us. Several of our kids worked together to help us pull off the move. I know the kids were surprised by where and how their grandpa lived (above a bar), but hopefully they saw the hope and promise for him in his new apartment. My sister and I just wanted Dad to take care of himself and his life. Was it really that much to ask of him?

Dad had his third episode of heart trouble and lung infection in 2011. This time it was much more complex, because we had to travel to get him the care he needed. Our dad was very fortunate that three of us were willing to help him once again, even though it took more time, more coordination, more money, and more time for Nancy and me away from our families and jobs. Bill had just started a new job so was unable to take his turn, which we all understood.

Seth's home and job were conveniently located between the clinic and Dad's place so he was a huge help during this time. When my sister and I first took Dad for his appointments, he was frail and weak. We were deeply concerned and just wanted to love him and get him through this crisis. After the first day of tests, we settled in our hotel room and Dad, who was exhausted, fell asleep. Nancy and I watched him sleeping peacefully and looked at one another as our eyes welled with tears. We were both thinking the same thoughts: was he too weak to overcome his problems? Could this time really be it? Time would tell.

We were amazed how quickly the clinic staff diagnosed Dad's condition and how to proceed. Along with their professionalism, we were impressed with their willingness to help someone in his situation. Dad has no money, no insurance and lives only on social security, but these doctors and nurses treated him respectfully, as if it didn't matter. We were relieved to learn that Dad didn't have cancer. He had a lung infection known as aspiration pneumonia, which would take time to clear up but necessary before they could begin to consider his heart valve surgery. From April to June, Dad did improve, but by his calls we knew he wasn't taking very good care of himself. By July he was cleared for the surgery but weeks before we questioned whether he would really go through with it. He was drinking a lot, probably because he was worried he wouldn't survive, but that was not helping the situation. When I made an inquiry on nursing-home care if needed following surgery, I discovered from his apartment manager that Dad was six months past due on rent. More reality: while we were all taking time from our families, my sister was covering his expenses with her hard-earned money, and we were taking time off work to get him back and forth, he was spending his income on his addictions as usual. He was still not taking responsibility for his own life.

I talked to Dad about it and he had his "same story different day" version of the manager actually owing him money. Of course this couldn't be his fault, and he gave a number of excuses for why it was the manager who had the problem and not him. Before the surgery that summer Dad gave the apartment manager his notice to vacate. My sister and I were sick, because we knew it would be impossible to find anything so ideal. It was unlikely that another assisted living program would take him in, especially because the manager was more concerned about Dad's noncompliance to following the rules than the past due rent. We decided that he would have to find a place to live himself if and when he recovered from surgery.

We were both very upset with Dad and told him so. He even went so far as to tell my sister, "As far as I am concerned, you are no longer my daughter." She called me in tears and said, "I am done." She had finally reached her breaking point. She even broke down and apologized to me for not being there for me through my separation and divorce. She now understood that it doesn't matter what we do; the alcoholics don't get it and definitely don't appreciate it. They just keep taking advantage of us. I told her I understood—the *disease* had taken its toll on her too. I told her that I know she loves me, and that she just didn't have enough left give which is OK—others stepped up to the plate. I am so glad that we had this breakthrough. I needed it to strengthen the sisterhood we shared. We decided getting Dad through surgery was the last thing we would do for him, then the rest of his life was up to him, including how he would move and where he would live. When would we get it? We had to finally just let go and let God.

The night before surgery, Dad was supposed to call the hospital to find out when to be there. At first, Nancy couldn't reach him. When she did finally, he was very drunk and said he couldn't get through to the hospital. She took over, got the information and gave it to our brother Seth, who was planning to pick Dad up early the next morning and get him to the hospital for the tests and surgery prep. When my brother got there, some guy was asleep in the apartment. He got to see the same story, different day and Dad still breaking the rules. They left the sleeping man in the apartment and made their way to the hospital to check-in on time.

My sister and I were able to travel together, just the two of us, to be there for Dad's surgery. We needed the time together and, as always, we needed one another through one more difficult life event, especially if things didn't go well. Dad, however, no matter how rough the first 24 hours were, managed to pull out of this one too. Did he realize the size of the gift these medical professionals had given him? He recovered well and later his friends helped him move. He lives with them now with what few possessions he has stored in another friend's garage. Age 73 and homeless. It is so very sad but we couldn't go through it again and what good would it do? Anything we arranged would only be temporary, because Dad wanted to live his way and not by the rules. Any time Dad calls these days, he is usually drinking at the bar or somewhere else. Most plans for him to visit have fallen through and he has been without his cell phone service often, a frequent occurrence over the years. So here we are stranded on base—same story, different day. Recently my sister received a bill for that past due rent. She sent it back to the manager with Dad's forwarding address and sent Dad a copy. It is his problem, not hers. She is letting go and letting God.

Why does Dad continue to live this way? How do I explain it to my 12-year old so he doesn't continue to be disappointed? I guess the "no expectations" idea is best. Why doesn't my brother Bill have more contact with us? I miss him and the boys miss their uncle. Why do I still wish my former husband would spend more time with his sons and why do I continue to push for it? Why is it so important to me and not to him? The answer is most likely because I want more for my kids than what I had when it comes to a father. Why can't my former husband just do what responsible dads do? Why doesn't he want to spend time with his kids, work hard like everyone else, pay his bills, and pay the child support in a timely manner? These are all good questions. But I have to remember it won't be easy to find answers with reason. Alcoholism makes life unreasonable on so many levels.

Isaiah 58:6-12

[6] "Is not this the kind of fasting I have chosen:
to loosen the chains of injustice
and untie the cords of the yoke,
to set the oppressed free
and break every yoke?
[7] Is it not to share your food with the hungry

and to provide the poor wanderer with shelter—
when you see the naked, to clothe them,
and not to turn away from your own flesh and blood?
[8] Then your light will break forth like the dawn,

and your healing will quickly appear;
then your righteousness[a] will go before you,
and the glory of the LORD will be your rear guard.
[9] Then you will call, and the LORD will answer;
you will cry for help, and he will say: Here am I.

"If you do away with the yoke of oppression,
with the pointing finger and malicious talk,
[10] and if you spend yourselves in behalf of the hungry
and satisfy the needs of the oppressed,
then your light will rise in the darkness,
and your night will become like the noonday.
[11] The LORD will guide you always;
he will satisfy your needs in a sun-scorched land
and will strengthen your frame.
You will be like a well-watered garden,
like a spring whose waters never fail.
[12] Your people will rebuild the ancient ruins
and will raise up the age-old foundations;
you will be called Repairer of Broken Walls,
Restorer of Streets with Dwellings. (Biblica).

CHAPTER 8

Home Run—My Recovery

God often puts appropriate people in your life when you need them most. I had known Tami in passing as a mom of four who had children similar in ages to mine and they all went to our neighborhood school, middle school and senior high school. God directed her to reach out to me the year of my divorce by inviting me to join in a Bible study with her and another friend. We didn't know each other that well, but I needed all the help I could get to be strong, so I accepted. Our group was small and the third person actually only came to one session because of her own difficult life situation. So Tami and I began on a journey with just the two of us quietly and spiritually in her home or out for lunch. We shared thoughts, tears, hugs, the Bible, our study, and prayer, and we both grew as Christians immensely.

It was the year that both of our oldest sons were graduating from high school so we shared a lot about that stage of our lives and all the changes that were ahead because of the milestone. We talked openly about our relationships and we often prayed for Jack. Many times I wondered if he had any idea how many people were not only there for me and the boys, but for him too. Tami and her family have strong faith and had reached out to the friend who started our Bible study with us but didn't finish. Tami also had a family member going through divorce so we prayed for them as well. Many of Jack's friends reached out to him too, but he would only talk about how he should do this or should do that but he never crossed the line or stepped up to the plate.

The Bible study Tami and I worked on was called *Breaking Free* (Moore, Beth) (excerpts below). It was incredibly powerful, and sharing it with someone was even more beneficial. Although our lives were busy and it was hard to make the time to review our study, we stayed committed. When we finished we were so proud of ourselves. I looked forward to every aspect of our time of study and reflection and I appreciated Tami so much for reaching out to me in my time of need. I learned so much from her, the study, my faith and God. In one exercise I learned not only how important it is to tear down the lies, but to be able to rebuild the truth. Perhaps the quality of honesty that I inherited from Grandpa made this really hit home for me, and made it important to help me move forward. I was so buried in the lies: that my marriage was fine, that we were all happy, and that our financial situation was going to improve. I had to get my life back and that meant breaking down the lies AND putting up the truth, rediscovering the person I really was. This was Step 9 of my 12-step program: "Made direct amends to such people wherever possible, except when to do so would injure them or others."

The last lesson of the study was so powerful that when I saw how it all tied together to what I had been through and to my life, I cried and cried. They were tears of so many different emotions. I felt sadness for all that my siblings and I missed out on because of the absence of our father in our lives. I felt the same sadness for what my nephews went through and still do struggle with because of their father's disease. I cried more tears for those same things for my own kids, the next generation, going through it too. I cried for the heartbreak we as a family endured instead of the happily ever after tale. The tears were like the rain pouring down on the field of my life. They were tears for all those who didn't step up to the plate and for all those that did. They were tears for my family, generations of it who went through heartache caused by the disease of alcoholism. They were tears for my recovery—my home run! All that I had been asking for was stated right there in the lesson "I pray for God's power to be revealed and I pray for Him to work out my circumstances. I pray for His direction and I pray for His favor. But more than anything on earth, I pray to know Him." (Moore, Beth). After sharing the revelation with my Aunt Penny she told me that she knew God was looking down proudly on me and I believed it. I felt it because He had been with me throughout the whole game.

The effect the study had on me was amazing; by the time I finished, I understood more fully why God wanted me to complete it. Perhaps the reason it took us five months to complete rather than ten weeks was because I needed the time to blend the study with my recovery. Little did we know God probably had it planned just so. I told Tami that I always had faith in God, but the Bible study and what I have been through assured me that my faith was the right place to turn, down to the blessing of the house sale just months after the divorce. Some excerpts from *Breaking Free* will stay with me forever "The display of His presence . . . God can plant us deeply in His love, grow us by the water of his word, and call us oaks of righteousness. We can be called persons of honesty, integrity, and liberation. As you can see from the definition, these results come only to those who have allowed God to create in each of them a new and clean heart" (Moore, Beth). My heart was so deeply dirtied by losing the love of my life, my hopes and dreams of raising our family together, and not being able to be together forever. It needed cleansing. No one can truly know the depth of the loneliness unless they have been there themselves. I felt so empty so many times. I cried myself to sleep night after night for months and months. That is often still the hardest time for me—going to bed at night—alone.

"Healing begins when we recognize how vulnerable those empty places make us, tally the cost of filling them with useless things, and seek wholeness in Christ alone. Wholeness in Christ is that state of being when every hole has been filled by Christ. The damage cannot be undone. It must be healed. The holes can't be taken away, but they can be filled. As you look at satisfaction in Christ, our goal is to see satisfaction at its greatest beauty. We want to see a picture of a satisfied person fully displaying God's splendor" (Moore, Beth).

The generations of alcoholism in my family were the ancient ruins, the rubble of my past, my childhood, my young adulthood, and the years of my marriage that I had lived through even more alcoholism. It was time to build anew. I was in a dark place and emotionally full of holes, an analogy similar to Isaiah 58:6-12. But during the worst times, God poured His love into those holes to bring me up to a level at which I could accept faith, family and friends to help me get through the toughest phases. Today I can be proud that the holes are filling up. I am building a new life for myself and I continue to enjoy my greatest gift: motherhood. By selling the house and paying down debts and living peacefully, I have a more manageable life. Comfort beyond that will take more time and patience and continued strength. I have faith that my wholeness will return and I will find overall happiness again one day—maybe even love. The damage cannot be undone, but it can be healed. The holes can't be taken away, but they can be filled.

Tami is good at writing and reflection. One day after we studied God's truths, she wrote about my comment "until you have experienced God's glory, you don't know that it is worth reflecting." She went on to explain that we do stumble and fall in life and feel alone but **God never fails us or leaves us**. She described shattering pain but **God's ability to strengthen**. She included one thought that I really love: despite the demands and screams in life that take all of our attention, **God's peace quiets us**. She talked of God's presence allowing us to persevere. She had seen that I had been through a difficult time, but that I went to the right place for my healing and even remembered to **thank God for the grace of his glory**. Reflecting is so rewarding and she played a huge role in helping me do so. This was Step 10 of my 12-step program: "Continued to take personal inventory, and when we were wrong, promptly admitted it."

Blessings in my life kept popping up all over the place. A simple gift from my coworker Kate inspired even more healing in me. One day she brought me a pretty pad of paper and matching pen. The heading on the notepad was GOD—GRACE—GRATITUDE. The words stuck with me awhile and then God spoke to me by helping me figure out what to do with them. Kate's warmth in that gift led me to start my own blog, where I kept writing about all the transition after the divorce using God—Grace—Gratitude as my general theme. I wrote about the few highs and many lows. I wrote about my relationships with my sons, with my family and friends, how I had grown in my faith and recovery, and about the lessons learned in those most difficult months and years of separation and divorce. Many of these are included in this book and helped in my recovery. Putting it all down in writing made me realize the deep effect alcoholism has had on my life even though I wasn't the one with the addiction.

Trusting God was the biggest thing that saved me. It was hard not to get discouraged but by trusting God I was able to gain strength and keep finding a way around the bases. I learned that by being honest and true to myself and living in reality, I could make my life manageable again and could even be happy. It isn't that I wasn't happy for most of my married life but the dreaded *disease* that kept following me through the men in my lives had taken over once again. I had lost myself and it was impairing my ability to be a good mother. Trusting **GOD** gave me courage and His **GRACE** helped me realize that despite all I was losing, I still had so much to be thankful for: **GRATITUDE!**

Staying on track was another way for me to move uphill and to heal. God guided me, filled my soul and kept my face toward the sun on the new path. I put daily focus on the most important matters first and life became manageable. The unmanageable path I had left behind was going downhill in alcoholism, debt, distrust, dishonesty, depression and despair. With each inning of the game I was playing, I gained more peace and that gave my heart the assurance to stay on track. This was Step 11 of my 12-step program: "Sought through prayer and meditation to improve our conscious contact with God *as we understood Him*, praying only for knowledge of His will for us and the power to carry that out."

1 Corinthians 13:4-7

[4] Love is patient, love is kind. It does not envy, it does not boast, it is not proud. [5] It does not dishonor others, it is not self-seeking, it is not easily angered, it keeps no record of wrongs. [6] Love does not delight in evil but rejoices with the truth. [7] It always protects, always trusts, always hopes, always perseveres. (Biblica)

I believe that part of my healing or being restored was realizing that even love wasn't enough to save my marriage, or my relationships with my brother and dad or my stepfather when he was living. I thought a lot about 1 Corinthians 13:4-7 and this realization. Love should be patient and kind, not arrogant and rude, nor dishonoring. It shouldn't insist on its own way but a way together. Love in relationships should bring rejoicing in truth and it should be enough to bear, believe, hope and endure all things. I keep hope in my heart that my next love will be all of those things. I also hope I can have Dad in my life happily and not stressfully somehow. And I pray that someday I get a warm loving relationship back with Bill and that my sons will know him like they used to when they were young and he was the family favorite team player. I will always hope that my former husband is close to our sons and that when it relates to them, we can always come together, that is one thing we have accomplished so far. Hopefully, by stepping up to the plate and embracing the lessons I learned through these nine innings, I have taught my sons this important lesson of love described in 1st Corinthians 13:4-7. I hope they learn to become loving men, wonderful husbands and fathers because of steps up to the plate I have taken for them.

One fall day on my blog, I wrote about how much I missed our yard and house after the move. But I decided maybe God created the seasons to help us adapt to change. Change is a part of life—children grow, relationships end, but a season always brings us something new. GRACE is defined in Scripture as "something that teaches us how to live!" God shows us grace in the changing of the seasons and we can adapt to changes in our lives by living in His grace.

Isaiah 61:1-4

The Year of the LORD's Favor
[1] The Spirit of the Sovereign LORD is on me,
because the LORD has anointed me
to proclaim good news to the poor.
He has sent me to bind up the brokenhearted,
to proclaim freedom for the captives
and release from darkness for the prisoners,[a]
[2] to proclaim the year of the LORD's favor
and the day of vengeance of our God,
to comfort all who mourn,
[3] and provide for those who grieve in Zion—
to bestow on them a crown of beauty
instead of ashes,
the oil of joy
instead of mourning,
and a garment of praise
instead of a spirit of despair.
They will be called oaks of righteousness,
a planting of the LORD
for the display of his splendor.
[4] They will rebuild the ancient ruins
and restore the places long devastated;
they will renew the ruined cities
that have been devastated for generations. (Biblica).

CHAPTER 9

Bottom of the 9th—Seeing Clearly

THE SERENITY PRAYER—"God grant me the serenity to accept the things I cannot change; courage to change the things I can; and wisdom to know the difference." (One Day at a Time in Al-Anon)

I have talked so much of the lack of reality in my life before separation and divorce and how I couldn't live it any more. I read *The Glass Castle* (Walls, Jeanette) at the recommendation of my sister in the summer of 2011. It was powerful and moving and familiar, fortunately not to the extremes in the book. It made me realize that the most of my father's life has been lived by that concept: ". . . someday I will build that glass castle or someday things will be better." I really miss my brother Bill, his distance from our family since his break in his sobriety shows we are not a priority in his life. His family seems to be his bar friends, just like our dad. The book also reaffirmed to me that I couldn't wait for my husband of 21 years to change, he didn't want to, so I had to see clearly for myself and my sons—for our emotional, financial and family future. I continue to pray that Jack finds a way to manage his life and live in a healthy way. It would help him, our kids and me; we could keep rebuilding. Maybe there will come a day where he does live manageably on his own, without my requests for payments or suggestions to pay things on time to improve his (our) credit, and most importantly to savor the relationships with our blessed sons. By seeing all we have been through, maybe the best thing of all will be for our sons to learn the lessons well and not repeat our mistakes. That is my hope for their entire generation in this family plagued with alcoholism—that they have the wisdom needed to not let it grab hold of them too.

I had so much frustration with Jack's lack of reality and lack of response by putting things off all the way through the divorce process. He actually told friends in the beginning of our separation that he wanted to take a year off from marriage, take in all the seasons and then come back. My friends agreed with me that he would have been asking too much. Hadn't I already tried to give him all the chances in the world to step up to the plate? He was shocked when I filed for divorce while he was still having fun experiencing the seasons! He didn't want reality or to see things clearly so we were forced to go to mediation to resolve matters, which were basically who took responsibility for which parts of our debt. If the house sale hadn't hit before the projected court date, we probably would have been forced there months later too. Just recently Jack moved into a place of his own. He had been staying with a friend for free for two and half years since leaving me. I often thought it was so unfair for him to be receiving that perk when I was the one raising the kids. From the beginning he didn't fight me on that. He knew I had been the one caring for them all along and always wanted to do so, but it still made me sad that he didn't want or make time to have regular visits with our sons. I continue to admire dads who do step up to the plate and are very involved in raising their children. If I ask or push Jack, he will do things for our kids, but that is the most I can expect from him. I know he is still hurting and I continue to pray for him. But I cannot be the person to help him; he has to step up to the plate and help himself.

The Glass Castle (Walls, Jeanette) was a great portrayal of how alcoholics perceive their lives (through the hope of building the glass castle that will never be) and what family members do to either cope or break free from that way of life. Some spouses or family members choose to live or stay in the insanity and keep their relationships with the alcoholic no matter what the cost. Some don't. I believe that is why both Alcoholics Anonymous and Al-Anon teach alcoholics and their families to live by the Serenity Prayer. We as the family members of alcoholics have to decide what is best for us, what we have in us and what we do with it. Do we have the courage to change what is within our power? Do we have the strength to face reality at all costs and move on? The alcoholics live their lives for themselves **first.** *Why shouldn't we?* I understand that it is a personal choice and that what is right for one person may not be for another.

While driving to work one morning after again waking up alone, I had an epiphany: I suddenly saw clearly why I so desperately want to be loved by a man "happily ever after." Most of the men in my life have continually let me down. Dad never stepped up to the plate to fill his fatherly role which has to be part of the void I feel. Dean did some. My early marriage was happy and loving but the disappointment came as our children got older and life priorities for Jack didn't match mine. I always had to be the responsible parent and I longed for a loving partnership. Not having a father or husband to count in this game of life has been hard. And I feel such distance from Bill and I would prefer to have my brother on home plate with me and not so far away in left field.

I know now that alcoholism has been part of my entire life, through generations, and I couldn't hold out any longer. I threw the opening pitch, shattering the glass castle (symbol from Chapter 1) to understand why my dad left us. I still love my family and know whose love I can count on, especially from God. I recognized the familiar patterns of the men in my life and have found a way to work through the line drives to my heart. I hit one out of the park by facing reality—to break down the ancient ruins that for me were the generations of alcoholism in my family. I began to take advantage of those pinch runners God sent to carry me through my separation and divorce and to help me know how to rebuild and restore myself and my life. I stepped back to see that my actions weren't going to change anyone from their same story, different day life. I grew from my own recovery and can focus on my future and that of my sons. I had to let go and let God when it came to all the alcoholic men in my life. My reality is my trust in God and in my faith, family and friends. At the end of the game, I understand that I have learned to know God as my MVP and that is my victory. He will continue to show His grace in my life and I will continue to have gratitude for every blessing bestowed upon me. This is Step 12 of my 12-step program: "Having had a spiritual awakening as the result of these steps, we tried to carry this message to alcoholics, and to practice these principles in all our affairs."

—Psalm 16:11

"You show me the path of life. In your presence there is fullness of joy." (Biblica).

S E R E N I T Y

```
O      V      E             N             O             N             H                    O
N      E      S             D                           E                                  U
S      R      P                           E             G
       Y      E             TO            X             O             J                    A
I      D      C                           P             D             O                    R
       A      T             I             E                           Y                    E
LOVE   Y      F             N             C             I
              U             S             T                           OF        STRONG
LIFE          L             A             A             TRUST
              N             T                           FAITH
       HOME   I             T                           FAMILY
              Y             O                           &
                            N                           FRIENDS
                            S
```

TWELVE STEPS

These are the original Twelve Steps as published by Alcoholics Anonymous which are also used by Al-Anon:

1. We admitted we were powerless over alcohol—that our lives had become unmanageable.
2. Came to believe that a Power greater than ourselves could restore us to sanity.
3. Made a decision to turn our will and our lives over to the care of God *as we understood Him.*
4. Made a searching and fearless moral inventory of ourselves.
5. Admitted to God, to ourselves, and to another human being the exact nature of our wrongs.
6. Were entirely ready to have God remove all these defects of character.
7. Humbly asked Him to remove our shortcomings.
8. Made a list of all persons we had harmed, and became willing to make amends to them all.
9. Made direct amends to such people wherever possible, except when to do so would injure them or others.
10. Continued to take personal inventory, and when we were wrong, promptly admitted it.
11. Sought through prayer and meditation to improve our conscious contact with God *as we understood Him,* praying only for knowledge of His will for us and the power to carry that out.
12. Having had a spiritual awakening as the result of these steps, we tried to carry this message to alcoholics, and to practice these principles in all our affairs.

http://en.wikipedia.org/wiki/Twelve-step_program

REFERENCES

Biblica. (2011). *Bible* New International Version (NIV). Website: www.biblegateway.com.

Courage to Change. One Day at a Time in Al-Anon II. (1992). Virginia Beach, VA: Al-Anon Family Group Headquarters, Inc.

Daily Word. (2008, 2009, 2010) Website: www.dailyword.com

Moore, Beth. (September 2006). *Breaking Free: Making Liberty in Christ a Reality in Life.* Nashville, TN: LifeWay Press.

My Utmost for His Highest. (2010). Website: www.utmost.org

One Day at a Time in Al-Anon. (2000). Virginia Beach, VA: Al-Anon Family Group Headquarters, Inc.

Victorious Deliverance Ministries. (2006).

Walls, Jeannette. *The Glass Castle: A Memoir.* (2005). New York, NY: Scribner.

Wikipedia. (2011). Website: www.wikipedia.org